D0397827

NOTE TO PARENTS

Welcome to Kingfisher Readers! This program is designed to help young readers build skills, confidence, and a love of reading as they explore their favorite topics.

These tips can help you get more from the experience of reading books together. But remember, the most important thing is to make reading fun!

Tips to Warm Up Before Reading

- Look through the book with your child. Ask them what they notice about the pictures.
- Wonder aloud together. Ask questions and make predictions. What will this book be about? What are some words we could expect to find on these pages?

While Reading

- Take turns or read together until your child takes over.
- Point to the words as you say them.
- When your child gets stuck on a word, ask if the picture could help. Then think about the first letter too.
- Accept and praise your child's contributions.

After Reading

- Look back at the things your child found interesting. Encourage connections to other things you both know.
- Draw pictures or make models to explore these ideas.
- Read the book again soon, to build fluency.

With five distinct levels and a wealth of appealing topics, the Kingfisher Readers series provides children with an exciting way to learn to read about the world around them. Enjoy!

Ellie Costa, M.S. Ed.
Literacy Specialist, Bank Street School for Children, New York

KINGFISHER READERS

level 2

Where Animals Live

Brenda Stones and
Thea Feldman

KINGFISHER
NEW YORK

KINGFISHER
LONDON & NEW YORK

Copyright © Kingfisher 2012
Published in the United States by Kingfisher,
175 Fifth Ave., New York, NY 10010
Kingfisher is an imprint of Macmillan Children's Books, London.
All rights reserved.

Distributed in the U.S. and Canada by Macmillan,
175 Fifth Ave., New York, NY 10010

Library of Congress Cataloging-in-Publication data
has been applied for.

Series editor: Thea Feldman
Literacy consultant: Ellie Costa, Bank St. College, New York

ISBN: 978-0-7534-6877-7 (HB)
ISBN: 978-0-7534-6878-4 (PB)

Kingfisher books are available for special promotions
and premiums. For details contact: Special Markets
Department, Macmillan, 175 Fifth Ave., New York, NY 10010.

For more information, please visit
www.kingfisherbooks.com

Printed in China
9 8 7 6 5 4 3 2 1
1TR/0712/UG/WKT/105MA

5044 7944 2/13

Picture credits
The Publisher would like to thank the following for permission to reproduce their material. Every care has
been taken to trace copyright holders. However, if there have been unintentional omissions or failure to trace
copyright holders, we apologize and will, if informed, endeavor to make corrections in any future edition.
Top = t; Bottom = b; Center = c; Left = l; Right = r
Cover Shutterstock (SS)/RCPPHOTO; Pages 4 SS/Pichuigin Dmitry; 5t SS/Jill Battglio; 5b SS/Hannamariah;
6–7 Photolibrary; 7 FLPA/Yva Momatiuk & John Eastcott; 8 SS/Nik Nikiz; 9 FLPA/ZSSD/Minden; 10 FLPA/
Panada Photo; 11 SS/Vladimir Chernyansky; 12–13 SS/MTrebbin; 13t SS/Tramper; 14–15 SS/alterfalter;
15 SS/Kristof Degreef; 16 SS/Robert Hackett; 17t SS/Anne Kitzman; 17b FLPA/Imagebroker; 18t SS/Johan
Sanepoel; 18b SS/Four Oaks; 19 SS/Joy Brown; 20 Nature PL/Kim Taylor; 21 SS/Krisvosheev Vitaly;
22 SS/Mikhail Olykainan; 23 Alamy/Chris Howes; 24 SS/janr34; 25t SS/Studiotouch; 25b SS/Indric;
26–27 Photolibrary; 27 SS/Cathy Keifer; 28 Photolibrary; 29 Photolibrary/Usher D; 30 SS/Graham Taylor;
31t Alamy/Kevin Foy; 31b SS/RCPPHOTO.

Contents

Home, sweet home!

Every wild animal needs
a place to live.

The place an animal lives
is called a **habitat**.

A habitat is an animal's home.

A seal's home is by the sea.

Some animals
live in **nests**
in trees.

Some animals
live underground.

Let's visit
more animals
at home!

Penguins

The South Pole is the coldest place on Earth.

But many penguins live there.

Special feathers keep them warm in the water and on land.

Penguins lay eggs on land.

The father Emperor penguin
balances the egg on his feet.

It stays warm there
until it hatches.

Polar bears

The North Pole is very cold too.

Polar bears live there.

Big paws help them walk on ice.

A polar bear digs a **snow den** before she gives birth to cubs.

Snow packed around the den keeps everyone warm and cozy!

Foxes

Where do foxes live?

They live in fields and woods.

But you might not see them.

They sleep during the day.

Foxes hunt for food at night.

Sometimes they come into towns to look for food.

You might see one then.

Moles

Look at these piles of dirt.

Where did they come from?

From a mole's home!

A mole lives underground.

He digs his home, and tunnels too.

A mole's home is called a **burrow**.

How does a mole dig a burrow?

With his sharp claws and teeth.

Chimpanzees

Many animals spend time high above the ground.

Chimpanzees sleep in nests in trees in forests in Africa.

A chimp learns to
build a nest
when she is young.

Chimps build
new nests
every night.

Squirrels

Squirrels live in trees too.

They live in woods, parks,
        and gardens.

A squirrel climbs
a tree with
    her sharp claws.

Her tail helps
her to balance.

A squirrel builds
a nest in a tree too.

It is called a **drey**.

A drey is made of
twigs, leaves,
and warm **moss**.

Baby squirrels sleeping in a drey

Bird nests

Many birds build nests when it is time to lay eggs.

The weaverbird is named for the amazing nests it weaves from leaves.

This swan nest has five eggs.

The mother will sit on the eggs.

The father will chase away
other animals.

Swallows

Some animals live in two places.

This swallow lives in one place when the weather is warm.

When it gets cold she flies away.

She flies to her second home.

It is in a warmer place.

Every summer the swallow flies
back to her first home.

She comes back to the same nest!

Ants

Many ants build a home together.

It is made of sticks and leaves.

It is called an **anthill**.

Thousands of ants
can live together
in one anthill!

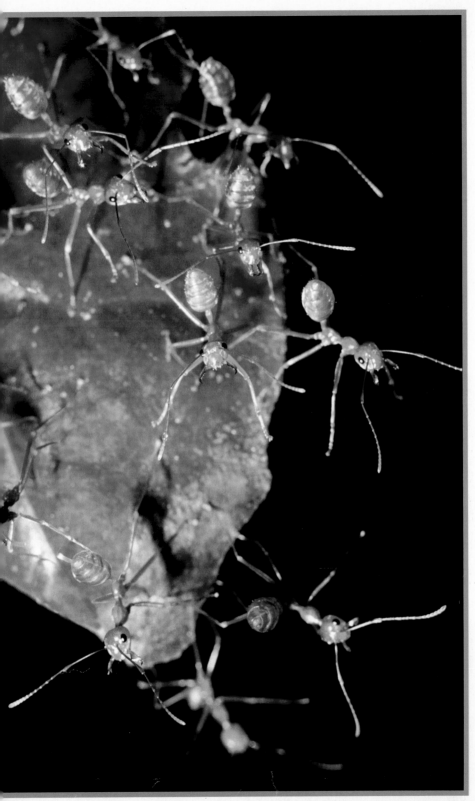

Wasps

Wasps build a home
together too.

They build a nest from
chewed bits of wood.

The nest is very strong.

The queen wasp lays eggs
in the nest.

Other wasps take care of the nest
and the eggs.

Butterflies

Butterflies seem so free!

But they need places to live too.

They live in places with flowers, such as fields and gardens.

Butterflies get food from flowers.

A butterfly lays eggs right on the leaves of plants!

Caterpillars grow in the eggs.

They hatch and stay on the leaves.

Safe at home

Wild animals live in many places.

They live in and by the sea.

They live in cold places.

They live in forests, parks, gardens, fields, and elsewhere.

It is up to us to take care
of all these places.

We need to
keep habitats safe
for animals
wherever
they live!

Glossary

anthill the home that many ants build together

burrow an underground home for some animals such as moles

drey the nest a squirrel builds in a tree

habitat the natural home for a wild animal

moss a kind of green plant that squirrels use in their nests

nests homes where some animals, such as squirrels, swallows, swans, and wasps, may live and raise young; also places chimpanzees build to sleep in each night

snow den a home dug in the snow

webs traps that some spiders spin to catch food

If you have enjoyed reading this book, look out for more in the Kingfisher Readers series!

KINGFISHER READERS: LEVEL 1

Baby Animals
Busy as a Bee
Butterflies
Colorful Coral Reefs
Jobs People Do
Seasons
Snakes Alive!
Trains

KINGFISHER READERS: LEVEL 2

What Animals Eat
Where Animals Live
Where We Live
Your Body

KINGFISHER READERS: LEVEL 3

Ancient Rome
Dinosaur World
Record Breakers—The Biggest
Volcanoes

KINGFISHER READERS: LEVEL 4

Flight
Pirates
Sharks
Weather

KINGFISHER READERS: LEVEL 5

Ancient Egyptians
Rainforests
Record Breakers—The Fastest
Space

For guidance for teachers and parents and activities and fun stuff for kids, go to the Kingfisher Readers website:
www.kingfisherreaders.com